FOR GOD

AND

COUNTRY

Fulton J. Sheen

Bishop Sheen Today
280 John Street
Midland, Ontario, Canada, L4R 2J5

www.bishopsheentoday.com

Library of Congress Cataloging-in-Publication Data
Names: Sheen, Fulton J. (Fulton John), 1895-1979, author. | Smith, Allan J., Editor.

Sheen, Fulton J. (Fulton John), 1895-1979. For God and Country. Registered in the name of P.J. Kenedy & Sons under Library of Congress catalog card number: A 153576, following publication May 8, 1941.

Title: For God and Country, Fulton J. Sheen,
author; edited by Allan J. Smith.

Description: Midland, Ontario: Bishop Sheen
Today, 2023.

Includes bibliographical references.

Identifiers:
ISBN: 978-1-990427-89-3 (paperback)
ISBN: 978-1-990427-91-6 (hardcover)
ISBN: 978-1-990427-90-9 (e-book)

Subjects: Anti-Christ - Sin – The Cross –
Liberal Thought – God

To Mary

**Immaculate Mother of God,
Gracious Queen of Christ's afflicted
ones, in prayerful petition
that the Glorious Peace of Christ
may reign in the souls of men.**

TABLE OF CONTENTS

INTRODUCTION

When looking back on the life of
Archbishop Fulton J. Sheen, there are some
that would refer to him as 'a man for all
seasons.' Over his lifetime, he spent himself
for souls, transforming lives with the clear
teaching of the truths of Christ and His
Church through his books, radio addresses,
lectures, television series, and many
newspaper columns.

Fulton J. Sheen was born in 1895 in El
Paso, Illinois. He lived and studied through a
time in history in which he witnessed the
effects of two world wars and many social,
political, and economic conflicts.

While a graduate student and university
professor in the United States and Europe,
Sheen made friends with a number of the
great thinkers and writers of his day such as
G.K. Chesterton, Christopher Dawson, J.R.R.
Tolkien, and C.S. Lewis.

After his ordination to the priesthood in
1919, Sheen would go on to receive numerous
degrees from the Catholic University of

America, Louvain University in Belgium, and the Angelicum University in Rome.

From 1926-1950 he was a full-time professor at the Catholic University of America, first in the School of Theology and later in the School of Philosophy. At the beginning of his teaching career, Sheen was regarded with esteem as one of the premier scholars of his time. The publication of his first book in 1925, *God and Intelligence in Modern Philosophy: A Critical Study in the Light of the Philosophy of Saint Thomas,* garnered Sheen extraordinary respect for his scholarship on St. Thomas Aquinas. The book was so well received that Sheen was awarded the Cardinal Mercier International Philosophy Award. Also impressed with the content was G.K. Chesterton, whose admiration is evidenced by his willingness to write the book's introduction.

During his time at the Catholic University of America, Sheen wrote thirty-four books on various topics. He also was the featured speaker on the Catholic Hour radio broadcast, having millions of listeners tuning in each week.

Witnessing the threat of Communism on the rise in the 1920s, it became sufficiently clear to Sheen that modern atheism was not only an esoteric philosophy preached by learned professors at Harvard and Yale, but it was a new type of Messianism emanating from Moscow, threatening to cover the face of the earth. So in the same year in which Pope Pius XI issued his encyclical on atheistic Communism (1937), Fulton J. Sheen published three books titled: *'Communism'*, *'Communism and Religion'*, and *'Liberty Under Communism'*.

Sheen stressed the need for the use of reason in dealing with Communism. On the subject matter, he was no intellectual featherweight, and he brought his formidable powers of intellect to bear on the problem of Communism, the better to refute it. He absorbed Marx, Lenin, and Stalin to prepare himself for the assaults he would sustain in his deconstruction of their theories. He was a tremendous success. He converted or influenced several Communists and leftists in the heyday of American Communism, including Louis Budenz, Elizabeth T. Bently, Bella Dodd, and Heywood Broun.

Toward the end of the 1930s, talk of war began to surface. When German forces invaded Poland on September 1, 1939, World War II began. Almost immediately Fulton J. Sheen rose to the occasion of being called to bring sense to a nation that was looking for answers to the questions of war. During his presentations on the radio he encouraged his audience to think of the great spiritual transformation that there would be in America if every Jew, Protestant, and Catholic according to the light of his conscience prayed one continuous hour a day, for the president, for Congress, and for victory.

Archbishop Sheen called World War II not only a political struggle, but also a 'theological one'. He referred to Hitler as an example of the "Anti-Christ." Sheen also said that, "the means of life no longer ministers to peace and order because we have perverted and forgotten the true ends of life... It is not our politics that has soured, nor our economics that have rusted; it is our hearts. We live and act as if God had never made us."

In 1941, the United States officially entered World War II. That same year Sheen penned the book *"A Declaration of Dependence."* In it, Sheen writes, "The Declaration of Independence, I repeat, is a Declaration of Dependence! We are independent of dictators because we are dependent on God. God is the necessary factor of our salvation. As a result, he is to be the center of our lives. His ways ought to permeate every aspect and area of our lives: education, employment, pleasure, mourning, socializing, etc. All is done in sight of the omnipotent Lord, and all we do should be done reflecting this knowledge. Our every interaction should be filled with the love of our Savior."

Numerous articles, radio reflections, and books would continue to be produced by Sheen throughout the war. Given their importance and the impact they had on society in his day, it seemed appropriate to re-release one of Sheen's best seminal works, *For God and Country* (New York: P.J. Kenedy and Sons, 1941).

The reflections contained in this work are a collection of Sheen's Catholic Hour radio addresses that were heard by millions of listeners each week. These reflections are a series of short essays that addressed the many concerns of the listeners of his day during the war.

Sheen answers questions about the Anti-Christ, hope, the four columns, the cross, and the power of God. His were some of the most clearly delineated investigations into the underlying causes of the war combined with an entirely sound and hopeful program for winning both the war and the even more important peace are found in them. These powerful reflections can be most heartily recommended for their wise counsel, sane and penetrating analysis, and logical conclusions.

Sheen writes, "There are two ways of looking at the war: one as a journalist, the other as a theologian. The journalist tells you what happens; the theologian not only why it happens, but also what matters. Our approach is from the divine point of view, first of all, because it is the only explanation which fits the facts; secondly, because the American people who have been confused by catchwords and slogans are seeking an inspiration for a total surrender of their great potentialities for sacrifice, both for God and country."

Sheen is firm in his conviction that real peace cannot be declared, it must be made. It is with peace-making and the fundamental conditions on which peace must be based that this book is concerned. In its seven forceful and readable chapters, it challenges the theory of many planners today who posture that military allies are necessarily political allies; it affirms that a common hatred can make nations allies, but only a common love can make them neighbors; it denies the primacy of action over reason, in the sense that the will of the state is that which makes a state right; and it contends that utility does not establish justice, but it is justice which makes utility.

With the same lucid and persuasive reasoning that has made him outstanding both as a writer and as a lecturer, Sheen continues to challenge people of goodwill to unite for the preservation of personal rights, freedom of conscience, human justice, and civilization itself – all of which are in danger in the present conflict. Here, one will recognize the urgency of Sheen's subject matter, and will find pillars of peace and promise in his far-sighted principles.

Archbishop Fulton J. Sheen's destiny was encrypted in his name, for in the Gaelic language *Fulton* means *war* and *Sheen* means *peace*. Sheen's lifelong goal was to establish peace, but in that call, he inevitably came up against many obstacles toward that noble ideal. It is as though his very name foretold the kind of life he was to have: an uninterrupted warring against the powers of darkness to promote the peace of Christ's kingdom.

ANTI-CHRIST

There is an inconsistency deeply rooted in our national life, which needs must be removed before America can exercise moral leadership among the nations. The inconsistency is between our education and our politics.

On the one hand, secular college and university education teaches in one form or another that there is no such thing as evil or guilt, that there are no absolute standards of right and wrong, that right and wrong depend entirely upon one's point of view.

On the other hand, the very products of this unmoral education are now, in the domain of politics, pointing their fingers at Hitler and Mussolini — not at Stalin, of course — and saying: "They are wicked; they are wrong; they are evil."

Naturally, we are tempted to ask: If right and wrong are relative to a point of view, then from Hitler's point of view he is right and we are wrong, and the only way to settle the dispute is by the methods of the jungle.

Furthermore, if there is no right and wrong, how could Hitler be wrong and how could we be right? If there is no black and white, why call the coal-black and the snow-white?

Our education denies moral standards while our politics affirms them, but only in particular instances. There is therefore a contradiction between the evil which the modern man would like to condemn in others, and his own denial of evil which his apostasy from God created.

He does not want to give up himself as the final standard of what is right and wrong, and yet sees that the same standard in others produced Hitler, the World War, and chaos.

Like a man who, when his wife awakens him saying she hears a burglar downstairs, insists violently that it is only her imagination, and yet goes downstairs trembling like a leaf fearful of bumping head-on with the marauder; so modern man, who says evil is only a survival of the imagination of medieval theologians, now shakes in fear from the evil he denied but which he knows in his heart to be only too real.

Modern man cannot go on in this inconsistency. He cannot keep his false education which denies guilt and his condemnation of Hitler and Mussolini as guilty. He cannot have it both ways.

But by trying to keep both, he utters such ridiculous judgments as that Hitler is an enemy when he invades the left side of Poland and Stalin is a friend when he invades the right.

Burglary is apparently wrong when you rob a stateroom on the starboard side of a ship, but positively friendly if you steal from the port side.

How shall we describe this abandonment of universal moral principles, except to say that we are stricken with a blindness such as it has been written will come upon all men before the end of time.

Just as the light of faith can be extinguished so that men no longer see the world through the eyes of Christ, so too the light of reason can be snuffed out, so that men no longer see right and wrong.

St. Paul told the Romans they had gone blind: "Because that, when they knew God, they have not glorified him as God, or given thanks; but because vain in their thoughts and their foolish heart was darkened" (Rom. 1:21).

Something like that has happened to the modern world and with perfect justice might Isaias say to us again: "Woe to you that call evil good, and good evil: that put darkness for light, and light for darkness: that put bitter for sweet, and sweet for bitter" (Isaiah 5:20).

Like those who have lost their physical vision, men give names to things which they no longer perceive. To real things we give false names; to false things, we give real names.

Words now refer not to things, but to myths or slogans in a confusion worse confounded than Babel.

In building the tower of Babel, men used different words to signify the same things and knew not what each other spoke; but today we use the same words but refer to different things.

At that time it was only tongues and ears that were confused; today it is the minds and souls of men.

With Hamlet who said to Polonius when asked: "What readest thou?" a de-Christianized culture can only answer:

"Words! Words! Words!" What is large we call small; what is small we call large.

Russia enthrones the cadaver of Lenin and the starving millions dance around the corpse and call it "life."

A word like "democracy" is used to support the anti-democratic, anti-Christian burning of ten thousand churches and chapels.

A word like "civil liberties" is used to de fend a violation of "civil liberties"; a word like "freedom" is used to mean absence of law, authority, and restraint.

When a professor teaches gross immorality to students or incites to revolution, we confuse the issue by speaking of "academic freedom."

When a Communist is arrested for sabotage, his fellow travelers call it "persecution."

When the Church pleads for the preservation of the family against artificial restriction of creative married love, the Church is called "reactionary."

The repudiation of intrinsic rights as the endowment of God is labeled by some of our jurists "Liberal."

The plea that nations invoke spiritual authority for the settlement of international issues is called "bringing the Pope to the White House."

The demand that children be released an hour a week from schools for religious and moral training is opposed not in the name of anti-religion — No! But in the name of education: "The child has not enough school time now to finish his important studies."

These same so-called educators who would pull their hair out if a child were given the wrong combination of colors on a toy are the very ones who teach the child there is no such thing as wrong.

What is this blindness which has so possessed us that we deny that evil exists and yet want to go to war to crush it? It is the blindness of the spirit of anti-Christ.

The spirit of anti-Christ is upon us, and it is part of our blindness to know it not. The greatest disaster that can happen to a man or a nation is not to do evil; it is to deny that evil exists by calling evil another name like "progress."

This is the unforgivable sin and the greatest of all sins, for if we deny we are wounded when our body bleeds, what need have we of healing?

We erroneously think that the spirit of anti-Christ should come with cloven hoofs and a tail, reeking with the smell of sulphur, with smoke belching from his ears and unmistakable green fumes vomiting from his mouth — a spectre so hideous that all men would shrink from him in terror and fright.

The Devil would not be wise if he came as the devil, for there is no deceit when evil wears no false face.

If we called vice "vice" and not "self-expression" who would be tempted?

Satan would have no appeal unless he clothed himself as an angel of light; hell would have no one knocking at its portals unless they were gilded with the gold of Paradise.

Christ comes to men with His cross that is why He has so few followers.

Satan comes without a cross, and not until victims are his do they know that the greatest cross in life is not to have the Cross.

Do not evil men disguise their evil; do not the Bolsheviks destroy Christianity in the name of "democracy"; does not Hitler destroy Poland in the name of "justice"; does not Mussolini invade Albania in the name of "protection"; do not the degenerate spread immorality in the name of "art"?

Shall the spirit of anti-Christ be less wise than his disciples?

Did not Our Lord speak of the devil as the "prince of this world"-certainly, princes are not frightening and particularly when they are princes of this world?

Did not Satan himself in tempting Our Lord say as he paraded the nations of the earth before the Savior's eyes: "... to me they are delivered, and to whom I will, I give them" (Luke 4:6-7).

Did not St. John say: "And it was given unto him to make war with the saints, and to overcome them. And power was given him over every tribe, and people, and tongue, and nation. And all that dwell upon the earth adored him, whose names are not written in the book of life of the Lamb, which was slain from the beginning of the world" (Rev. 13:7-8).

Something is rotten with the world; and that rottenness is so radical and universal that it can be explained not by things, but by a spirit — the spirit of evil.

It is our blindness not to know there is evil because we denied its existence. A man without eyes can be persuaded night is day and day is night.

So too the modern world which has lost both its eyes of faith and its eyes of reason can be made to believe the spirit of anti-Christ is not here, for having forgotten Christ, who shall persuade it there is an anti-Christ?

Our blindness is colossal and the root of our evil is our refusal to admit evil and sin. If only we admitted we were blind there would be hope, but hellish blindness thinks that it can see.

Men think that evil must come in the disguise of a germ, or a bomb, or a raid, or an explosion, or a train wreck, or a bank failure, forgetful that the greatest grief can come to man under the disguise of human ideals.

It is under the masquerade of a progress which denies sin and guilt that anti-Christ parades the world today, sits in our lecture rooms, writes in our magazines, struts across our stages, promising to redeem man when he has left the Cross and penance behind, but only completing man's enslavement when it is already too late for him to free himself.

There is a radical inconsistency in our way of life; that is, in our education which denies there is evil, and in our politics which says dictators are evil.

If there be no grime, who shall be called grimy? If there is no disease who shall be called sick? If there shall be no decay, who shall be called rotten?

The choice is not between an education which denies guilt and a politics which makes only dictators guilty. Both are false, and both must be scrapped in their present form.

Education which denies evil must be abandoned because it fails to make a distinction between an intellectual error and bad behavior.

If I add ten and ten to make thirty, I err, and an eraser can correct it; but if I tell a falsehood about my neighbor and ruin his reputation, I sin.

Modern education makes no distinction between error and sin; it teaches that what we call evil is only an intellectual error.

That is why it preaches that crime and antisocial behavior are due to mental immaturity. Only the ignorant sin; the intelligentsia can't sin — they know. Hence, educate everyone and evil will disappear.

The fact is, education does not take away evil because the training of the reason is quite distinct from the training of the will; knowing is not doing.

Modern education which trains only the mind takes away error — sometimes, but it does not train the will or take away sin.

Nothing is more destructive of our national life than this fallacy that the educated are sinless because they have an A.B., and that the uneducated are wrong because they never heard of Bertrand Russell.

The truth is rather the contrary, the uneducated in this country have less evil in them than the intelligentsia; they may make errors, but they commit less sin.

And on the Day of Judgment, it will be far better to be ignorant before the face of Almighty God than worldly-wise but sinful.

What is true of education which denies guilt is true of politics which identifies guilt with dictators. This is a very false morality.

First, because those who say that dictatorships are evil do not believe it. If dictatorship were wrong we would condemn it wherever we found it. Not all Americans believe an anti-God, anti-human dictatorship is wrong. If all did, they would not call Russia a "friendly nation."

Second, if the only evil in the world were dictatorships, would we be a moral world if the three were vanquished? Did the world become safe for democracy when the Kaiser went to Doorn? Would it be safe tomorrow if Hitler went to Canossa?

Dictators are not the only evils. They are more the creatures of evil than the creatures the creatures of godlessness, selfishness, and repudiation of morality, domestic, industrial, and international.

By limiting evil to dictatorships we take eyes off ourselves and thus delay that eradication of evil from our own lives which would strengthen us more than armaments, to defeat that evil from without.

This denial of evil as evil has hindered our moral development. Evil, when it is recognized as such and repented, leads a man to reach a higher degree of perfection.

Even the angels of heaven rejoice more at one sinner doing penance than ninety-nine just who need not penance. The recoil of repentance often summons forth energies in the opposite direction.

But if a man denies there is sickness, then how shall he make efforts to restore himself to health? If a man thinks he knows it all, whence shall come his energies to learn? If there be no evil, how shall we repent? How can we defeat evil unless we know it?

The condition of national peace is the scrapping both of false education and false politics, the former of which denies evil and the latter of which limits evil to dictatorships, environment, poor milk, or bad glands.

Evil is real; it is in the human heart; born first in man, then socialized in groups and society.

Like Bartimeus, the son of Timeus, who begged on the streets of Jericho, we too are blind. We really have eyes and see not.

We need the touch of a Savior who on His way to the Cross stops in His journey despite the rebuke of a crowd, and opens blind eyes to Redemption and Salvation.

God grant that we in America may see before it is too late. Today we are fearing the wrong thing. As Sacred Scripture says, we fear where there is no fear.

We fear the outside when we should fear the inside; we fear external dangers, but not the internal sins which produce collective ills.

We fear man, too, when we should fear God. Man today is afraid of his own kind. Lions do not fear lions; tigers do not fear tigers. They fear only that which is outside their species. But man fears man.

The capitalist fears the worker, the worker the capitalist, the poor fear the rich, the rich fear the poor — but no one fears God. If man only knew it, he fears man because he has ceased to fear God; for the man who has lost his roots in God is the terror of his fellowmen.

"The fear of the Lord is the beginning of wisdom" (Prov. 1:7) — only the beginning, for in later stages love replaces fear.

But in the beginning, we must fear justice for our injustice; retribution for our sins; consequences for our moral misdeeds. There will never be peace in this world so long as man fears man rather than God.

To fear God is not only to love God, but also to love one's fellowman.

We need a new kind of fear — not just a fear of the invader that strikes our shores, but a fear lest by denying there is evil, we become impotent to strike it; a fear that if we say all we need is bread, bread is all we will get — as if man could live by bread alone; a fear that by denying evil we will lose the ideal of goodness; a fear lest while protecting our boundaries, our inner citadels and our homes will be seized from within.

There are many reasons why we know evil is existent in the world; there are many reasons why we believe in the spirit of anti-Christ.

Our modern educators, and our press, by the denial of guilt, sin, evil, and penance, sacrifice and reparation have not convinced us there is no God; they have not convinced us of the futility of the Cross; they have not convinced us there is no evil.

But they have convinced us there is a Devil, for the Devil is never so triumphant as when he induces his followers to say there is no Devil!

THE REALITY OF SIN

George Bernard Shaw once said: the "modern man is too busy to think about his sins."

It perhaps would be truer to say the modern man denies that he can sin. In some so-called learned circles sin is explained away biologically as a "fall in the evolutionary process," or as a temporary, atavistic throwback to our animal ancestry "which man can overcome through proper mating."

Others explain it away "physically" by attributing moral aberrations to physical environment, lack of playgrounds, Grade A milk, and bad glands.

Evil is therefore not in the will, but in the bile, not in the soul, but in the organism; is physiological, not moral.

A third attempt to explain sin away is the social; sin is not personal but social. Evil is due not to violations of conscience, but to something external, e.g., the capitalists, in the case of Communists; the dictatorships, in the case of democracy; democracy in the case of dictatorship.

Evil is blamed on a system or on institutions, but never on the person. The distinction between right and wrong thus gives way to "ally" or "enemy."

As the world sins more it thinks less about it, a condition as dangerous for the soul as of indifference to germs in time of pestilence. A sense of drift has been substituted for a sense of sin.

The former acts like an opiate instilling into the soul an insidious acquiescence to evil which is supposed to reside in external circumstances and therefore beyond the victim's control.

Because the world assumes that evil is wholly external or social, it falsely believes that its remedy lies in the domain of politics and economics since they deal with the externals or with what a man has rather than what he is.

This very refusal to face the issue that sin is personal, and a moral rather than an economic phenomenon, makes a cure impossible. It puts society in the state of a man who thinks that his jaundice comes from the immigration of the yellow races and that a good alcohol rub or some fine face powder will cure it.

There can be no personal, no social salvation until the sense of sin is restored and evil is recognized not as something external, but also something within each of us.

In other words, the world is not in its present mess because something is out of gear, but rather because something is wrong.

Three disastrous consequences flow from the denial of personal sin and guilt: 1) Loss of freedom; 2) National paralysis; 3) Neurosis and frustration.

1) Loss of Freedom: There is nothing the modern man prizes more than freedom, but does he realize that his denial of sin is the denial of freedom? Does not freedom imply choice? Does not choice imply alternatives of good and evil?

If I do not sin when I choose the wrong alternative, then I am not responsible, but if I am not responsible then I am not free.

Cabbages, horses, adding machines, boots, ships, and sealing wax cannot sin, because they have no freedom, therefore no responsibility. To deny sin is therefore to reduce man to the status of a thing.

Incidentally, this is the basic philosophical reason for Fascism, Nazism, and Communism, for if man is only a thing and not a moral being, free and responsible, then why should he not be absorbed into the collectivity or totality of race as in Germany, class as in Russia, and the nation as in Italy?

We cannot have it both ways: if we are free, then we can do wrong; but if we cannot do wrong, then we are not free.

Our so-called liberal and progressive educators who denied the reality of guilt, did not, as they promised, relieve man from the shackles of "medieval morality"; but they did relieve the person of his responsibility and therefore of his freedom.

Freudian psychologists in democracies who blamed all sin or guilt on the psychical determinism of a sub-rational or even sexual factor, and the Marxian philosopher in totalitarian states who blamed sin on to the social determinism of the economic order, did not really explain away sin; but they did explain away freedom.

Men talk most about freedom when they are losing it, as they talk most about health when they are sick.

Real freedom is slipping away from the world today and the era foretold by Dostoevski is upon us: "The ages will come to pass, and humanity will proclaim by the lips of their sages that there is no crime; there is no sin; there is only hunger. In the end they will lay their freedom at our feet and say to us 'make us your slaves,' but feed us."

The denial that we could do wrong is the greatest wrong of all. The Devil was wiser than modern man, for the Devil tempted Adam and Eve to use their freedom falsely by eating of the fruit of the tree of the knowledge of good and evil.

Satan was never so stupid as to think that freedom meant irresponsibility. But he has so convinced his disciples in the 20th century! He promised freedom in the beginning by inciting to evil; he takes freedom away now by denying evil. And we in our ignorance call this progress!

2) National Paralysis: Once a nation begins to say: "There is no right or wrong, for as Einstein has proven everything is relative; virtue and vice are only questions of a point of

view," it, by that very fact, develops a false tolerance. I say, false tolerance because it identifies tolerance with indifference to right and wrong.

"Broadmindedness" then becomes praised as a great virtue, whereas in reality, it is nothing but flat headedness — an inability to see that mountains are high, valleys are low, virtue is right, vice is wrong.

If there is no evil, then how can we resist it? If there are no broken bones, then why call in a physician?

The refusal to recognize wrong as wrong delays or prevents all reactions to wrong. The fact is that if the doctors were as indifferent to disease and as broadminded about germs as the nation is as broadminded about right and wrong, America would have been ravaged long ago.

Some time ago I was invited to be on the committee of a rather well-known group in the United States. Among other reasons, I declined because that same group sponsored a much-publicized attack on religion by a rather well-known scientist.

An appeal was made to my broadmindedness. "After all, you would not be intolerant
would you?"

I asked this particular official if he had a
child? Admitting he had, I said: "Suppose your
child was taken seriously ill. Five doctors were
called in and all admitted that it was a
dangerous streptococcus infection. But three
of them said to you: 'We know that there are
rather intolerant specialists who say that a
streptococcus infection is dangerous, but after
all, this is only a point of view. What is healthy
and what is unhealthy is purely relative.
Personally, we think that you should be
broadminded about this germ, and allow us to
develop it, for we seem to have a particular
good culture in your child.'"

I then asked him: "What would you say to
those doctors?" He said: "I would order them
out, for the life of my child is worth more than
the life of a germ."

But I said: "Aren't you a bit intolerant? In
any case, if you consider the life of the soul,
more than the body, and the preservation of
inalienable rights of God as a gift of God more
precious than the feelings of an antireligious
scientist, why is it wrong for me to refuse to be
a member of a committee which sponsors
lectures destructive of democracy and the

country I love? If you are intolerant to a streptococcus germ which destroys a body, why should I not be intolerant about an evil which destroys the nation?"

Multiply this indifference to evil, sin, and wrong ten thousand times and there is created a national paralysis, that is, an inability to cope with anti-American activities because we no longer know what is good for America or bad for America.

Why, for example, is America incapable of dealing effectively with Fifth Columnists? Because asserting that freedom means the right to do whatever you please, instead of the right to do whatever you ought, it is unable to draw the line between right and wrong.

If Communism were a germ destroying the pigs on the American farms, our university professors would sit up nights seeking antidotes, but because in the social order we have nothing corresponding to a germ, in virtue of the denial of evil, we have some university professors sitting up nights seeking to find ways to keep them on the ballots to use our freedom in order to destroy it.

Even though they had no moral sense, America would be better off if these same defenders of Communism agreed only to give to Communists in America exactly the same rights they have in Russia.

Can we not see that by denying evil we are rendered impotent to cope with it? What is international appeasement to a great extent but a refusal to recognize the intrinsically evil intentions of men.

Appeasement is based on ignorance of evil. National leaders look to intellectual mistakes to account for moral perversity. Evil having no historic dimensions cannot be recognized.

It was such a national paralysis based on a denial of evil which made France trust Russia and which is making us trust Russia and call it "friendly."

There is no nation on earth that is so intolerant of germs as the United States; there are few nations which are so tolerant of evil and sin.

A pneumonia germ which as a Fifth Columnist gains entry into a body is immediately flanked by an army of surgeons, physicians, and scientists, but a Communist which as a Fifth Columnist penetrates into our labor unions and schools and our army, is flanked by Defenders of Civil Liberties, for if there be no wrong, why is he wrong?

One can lay down the general law that the greater the apathy to righteousness born of God in a nation, the greater is its danger of corruption from within.

3) Neurosis and Frustration: The denial of sin is at the base of much of the nervous disorders in the world today. Neurosis to a great extent is due to frustration.

Experiments made on rats prove that by being constantly frustrated in their search for food they went mad. Even pigs, who seem to be most immune from worry, were also driven crazy by similar frustration.

Modern man too is being constantly frustrated by unrealized purposes of expectation and realization of the prospect of a future joy and the unhappiness consequent upon its possession.

This is particularly true of those who, badly educated, are fated to continue in attempts to achieve happiness, which by their very nature, are doomed to end in despair.

Trying to make a heaven out of earth, to find pie in the sky, or happiness in evil and peace in violation of a moral law is like being condemned to be eternally fitting squares into round holes.

Nothing better illustrates this frustration than the modern attitude toward marriage, that is, between the expectation of romantic love and the reality of the state.

Practically all love songs on the radio center about those who are about to be married, e.g., "how happy we will be"; "will you be mine forever". But how often do we hear a love song on the radio about that same couple five years after marriage — if they are still married.

What do we hear instead? Jokes about marriage, most of which are only variations of that old bromide: "That was not a lady, that was my wife."

Why do we joke about marriage, if it be not to repress our deep disillusionment? As an Oriental explained: "Americans are not really happy — they laugh too much."

Not only is this frustration serious, but the escapes from it are worse, for in each instance modern man tries to find the escape in external circumstances; if he is married he thinks he would be happier if he had another wife; if he is a Communist, he thinks he would be happier if he were a Capitalist; if he is a Capitalist he thinks he could be happier if he were a "Fellow Traveller" — but all are destined to bring increased woe because the wrong in the heart cannot be relieved by another wrong in society.

Could we but see it, sin is unreasonableness and unreasonableness is destruction. It is an act against reason to jump from a roof, and if I do jump, I injure myself.

My reason tells me a pencil is to be used for writing; if I use it to open a door, I destroy the pencil. In like manner, reason and revelation both tell me my purpose and my happiness consist in the attainment of the Perfect Life, Truth, and Love which is God If I willfully rebel against the purpose I mutilate myself. And the constant frustration which comes of trying to open doors with pencils or to attain peace without morality intensifies psychoses and often ends in madness.

To escape this inner conflict modern man constantly seeks to fill the void which only God can fill. For that reason he hates repose; he wants to "kill time."

Existence in time cannot be endured; so he seeks to fly from it into a life where he can forget himself. Most of his pleasures are at bottom nothing else than a "pass-time" or a substitute for an empty soul. His music with its staccato discontinuity drives him on to a movement which goes nowhere but becomes a narcotic to "dope" his soul.

Nothing is as intolerable as being alone. He cannot stand himself; he almost hates himself and his nothingness and his failures. The virtuous man and woman is to him a reproach so he keeps them off with scorn.

His conscience carries on an unbearable repartee; his whole being becomes eccentric like a planet out of its course, burning itself out; he feels his name is "legion" for there are so many contradictory impulses within him; like a radio tuned in to two stations, he gets nothing but moral static; a veritable civil war rages in his soul and to silence it he loses himself in the crowd; anonymity almost becomes a law of his life.

He is no longer a person, he is one of a herd. When a frustrated man says he has a good conscience, he only means he has a bad memory. The bad conscience is like a dog which is shut up in the cellar because of the bad habit of continually barking, but which will bark more because the master ignored him.

This bad conscience, did man but recognize it, is the way sinners experience the presence of God. As the virtuous feel God in peace, the sinners do so in wrath.

"My conscience hath a thousand several tongues, and every tongue brings in a different tale: And every tale condemns me for a villain." (Richard III)

We may deny sin, but we cannot deny its consequences; they are still with us: a loss of freedom — as men deny responsibility, they surrender freedom; a national paralysis to meet barbarism —because we deny it is evil; a neurosis and a psychosis-induced from trying to find peace in anything short of Him for Whom we were made.

But our problem is: what shall we do with our sin? There are three escapes: 1) Keep the wound open; 2) Cover it over; 3) Heal it.

1) Keep the wound open: this is the remedy invoked by hypochondriacs who have an excessive interest in the symptoms of disease. They rush off to psychoanalysts to discover the source of their complex, and ninety-nine times out of a hundred, the psychoanalyst will tell them it has something to do with sex.

The patient likes to hear about sex as the origin of his psychosis, because it takes his mind off guilt. A sublimation is a thousand times easier to get than an absolution. So the wound is kept open because of a false diagnosis.

2) Cover it over: This second escape films over the guilt by rationalizing it, or by inventing false gods or idols. Certain cliques hide bad thinking, such as: "You don't really believe in sin." "Imagine anyone in these days of science believing in God." "You never heard of Bertrand Russell?" This treatment merely films over the ulcerous parts whilst rank corruption mining all within.

The souls which use this remedy are of the same type who run from bill collectors. Someday the collector will catch up with them.

The longer they put off the cure and repress the sense of guilt, the greater becomes their melancholy and despondency and the temptation to suicide.

3) Heal it: But in order to heal it two conditions must be fulfilled.

First, I must recognize the truth of the deliverances of my conscience, that sin is an offense against a Person, for it surrounds me with the same sense of guilt as if I had struck my own mother.

I feel as if I had made a false declaration of independence like the Prodigal Son. I feel disloyal to the purpose for which I was made, and this means disloyal to God. I feel like Adam who hid from God after his sin, by which he symbolized the distance a sinner feels from God.

My sin is not disrespectability, it is not fear of the loss of the good opinion of neighbors; it is rather a kind of anticipated death in which I feel the breakdown of the fellowship, not of soul and body, but of soul and God.

Secondly, since sin broke off my relations with the purpose of living and destroyed my freedom by making me the slave of sin, it follows that if ever I am to have peace, I must re-establish relations with that Person, which is God.

I must do it. Why? Because if God forces me to do it, He would destroy my nature. God cannot infringe upon man's freedom, for by so doing He would crush the very freedom that makes love possible.

So God, in order to win us, puts Himself in the attitude of one who is incapable of destroying freedom. He comes to us in a human nature on the Cross. Hands that are pinioned with nails cannot take us prisoner;

feet that are dug with steel cannot pursue. True love is always unarmed yet devoted unto sacrifice.

He can only solicit by presenting to us the picture of what the sin did to Him. He seeks to move us by the vision of a sacrifice of which He can say, "Greater love than this no man hath."

Very often the sight of the suffering which the drunkenness of a husband has brought upon a wife will break him of his habit; so too Our Lord hopes that the revelation of what our sins have done to Him will bring us to repentance.

The Crucifixion was not murder; it was deicide — the worst that sin can do. The very sight of His suffering is not only the measure of our guilt, it is at the same time the offer of forgiveness.

Through the Cross our guilt is transformed into sorrow at seeing its consequences — a poignant personal healing sorrow which tortures our soul until we cry out: "Lord, be merciful unto me a sinner."

From that cross, Love looked down, for by its nature Love descends. Parents love their children more than children love their parents.

In fact, children do not know how much their parents suffered for them until they become parents themselves. Love descends from the cross. We are too dumb to understand that love of the Cross because we are such strangers to sacrifice; we do not know what love is because we have not loved — we have only yearned.

Because we love so little, His love is mysterious to us. We never forgave anyone at such a cost as His; we never loved anyone at such a price as He did. Our own lovelessness has hidden Calvary.

Not until we begin to love Goodness will we understand how good God was to die for us. Sin is our fault! What are we going to do about it?

The world will explain it away; Our Lord will forgive it. He has conferred that power of forgiveness to His Church unto the consummation of the world: "Whose sins you shall forgive, they are forgiven them" (John 20:23). Thank God, I am a Catholic.

THE MASSES AND GOD

THE MASSES AND GOD

Wherein lies the future of America? The problem is concerned with a choice between two classes: The intelligentsia and the masses.

Our conclusion will be: The future of a better America is in the masses and not in the intelligentsia, for we are witnessing in our national life what might be called the Betrayal of the Intellectuals, or the Treason of the Educated.

Before giving reasons one must define terms. By the intelligentsia I mean the intellectuals who have been educated beyond their intelligence; those who deny absolute standards of right and wrong, make truth and error relative to a point of view, and completely ignore the will and its discipline in the training of youth.

Among specimens of the intelligentsia might be mentioned, H. G. Wells, George Bernard Shaw, John Dewey, and the new lawyers who teach ideas are instruments of power.

A few decades ago the influences which made our civilization, came from above, that is, from the educated. But today the influences which make civilization are coming not from above, but from below — from the masses. What happened to the rich in the last twelve years is now happening to the intelligentsia.

For a decade, we held up the ideal of wealth as the American ideal; we asked our young to look upon our millionaires as paragons of success and as models in the museum of Americana. But now all that has changed. The rich today are on the defensive. And why? Because they were not loyal to the stewardship of wealth; they thought wealth was something so personal as to be devoid of all social responsibilities.

In like manner, the intelligentsia today are on the defensive because they were not loyal to the stewardship of truth. In the pre-depression days of wealth, there was such a thing as "economic slumming": The rich went down to the poor, not to relieve themselves of their wealth, not to relieve the poor of their poverty, but to enjoy the shock and thrill of contrast.

In these days, the intelligentsia have gone slumming: University Professors go down to the masses not to give the masses truth, for they deny truth; not to relieve them of their ignorance by learned and virtuous leadership, for they say there is no right or wrong; but only to enjoy the shock and thrill of mass movement without intelligent direction. If there be no health, why have doctors? If power is not in Truth ask the masses, why should it not be in violence?

In one well-endowed American University, a professor said there was not a single student in his class who could give a rational justification for democracy; its justification was only its power to assert itself over rival forms.

The intelligentsia in our Universities were talking Utopian nonsense about Progress when the whole of Western Civilization was already facing its hour of doom. As a result, students became cynical.

In a novel of Dostoevski, a young son became more and more opposed to his father who lived in a world of Utopian illusions and who believed that the law of evolution would make a better and richer world.

The son realized that the world did not conform to his father's idea of progress and through corrosive cynicism finally ended by believing that nothing in life is worthwhile. A similar attitude is seizing many youths in Universities today.

Because the intelligentsia have missed the signs of the time, they have lost their authority. They are paying the penalty for their spiritual frigidity and their moral indifference because they lost the power to fulfill the tasks with which they are confronted.

Something similar happened in the days of the decline of pagan Rome. The intelligentsia had nothing more to offer the world: Their philosophy was only a history of conflicting views of life, and they threw away the precious heritage of reason at the very moment they most loudly shouted they lived by it and, by denying that liberty is inseparable from law, ceased to be sages and dropped to crankiness instead of rising to sainthood.

Our wise men today, like them, are not wise enough. Their prestige for impartiality and objectivity is only a false tolerance of right and wrong; they think a student is not learned unless he has counted something no one else has ever counted before, as one University in the West counted, and I am quoting the title of the P.H.D. thesis — "the microbic content of cotton undershirts" — while another University in the East counted all the datives in Ovid. Understanding became identified with measure, from which they conclude that the immeasurable is the unknowable, and the unknowable is the unreal.

God, the soul, and the supernatural life, are relegated to the domain of myths and fantasies; justice becomes a balance between conflicting opinions; morality a statistical average; and democracy an arithmocracy where a majority makes a thing right, even when a democracy decides to vote itself out of democracy.

Man becomes a spectator of reality, rather than its creator. He observes what goes on outside of him but never learns to connect what goes on inside of him.

Because Jerusalem was not faithful to its vocation, its kingdom was taken away and given to the Gentiles, so too, because the intelligentsia have been traitors to truth, their kingdom is being taken away and given to the masses.

As the betrayal of leadership among the intellectuals of pagan Rome threw the burden upon the mercenaries recruited from beyond the frontiers, so too the slumming of our intelligentsia has shifted the field of influence to the masses. They now hold the key that the educators threw away.

This is no tragedy. The cry of Frederick Ozanam who dedicated his life to them must therefore be renewed in our day: "Passions aux barbares" "Down to the masses," to the broken earthenware of humanity, to the socially disinherited, to those whose wants are too many and whose rights are too few, to those whom Edmund Burke contemptuously called the "great unwashed."

They are the hope of a better America and principally for these reasons: Because the masses are capable of far better judgments about world affairs than the intelligentsia.

If I wanted a good moral judgment about the war, I should a thousand times prefer to get it from a garage man, a filling station attendant, a WPA worker, a grocer's clerk, or a delivery boy, than from twenty-three Ph.D. Professors I know about in just one American University.

The reason is not difficult to find. The educated know how to rationalize evil; the masses do not. Evil to them is still evil; they have never learned to sugar-coat it with sophism. They never got enough smattering of Einstein to sophomorically pontificate, "everything is relative." If they do wrong, they still call it wrong. Their judgments are better because their moral sense is higher, for virtue does not increase in direct ratio with learning. Knowledge of things is no guarantee of knowledge of self.

And in saying this I am only repeating in poor language the eternally beautiful thought of the Savior: "I confess to thee, O Father, Lord of heaven and earth, because thou hast hidden these things from the wise and prudent and hast revealed them to little ones" (Luke 10:21).

Having little to defend economically, the masses are not so apt to identify justice with the present order of things. It is easy for the man who is comfortable to fall into the error of believing that any protest against his possessions is revolutionary. But for the masses justice is not the maintenance of the status quo, but an order which gives equal opportunity to all.

Their struggle for the economic necessities has convinced them that the good and just things must be re-captured from day to day: The lawyer must re-capture his profession by study; the priest by daily meditation; the government by the solution of new social problems; and even the fortress of life must be defended daily from disease and death.

The masses are the hope of the future for the potentialities of sacrifice, which is essential to the preservation of a nation in time of trouble, is greater in them than in the intelligentsia who too often think they are serving the nation when they are only indulging in sociological adventurism. It is character, not learning, that makes a nation great.

But character is in the will, not in the intellect. Even though the intelligentsia may know more, the will of the masses is greatly superior; and for that reason it is from the quarry of the common man that the stones of a great nation must be cut.

This point must be emphasized for it is too common today to identify moral worth with knowledge — a consequence perhaps of the denial of sins and the attribution of sin to ignorance.

How false this is, was strikingly emphasized on the occasion of one of Our Lord's visits to Jerusalem when a group of the intelligentsia affronted Him saying, "How doth this man know letters, having never learned?" (John 7:15).

They were of the same group who, when He gave them bread would have made Him King, but who when He said the bread He gave was from heaven, left Him and walked no more with Him.

Now again they were impressed not by what He did to a man morally, but by His "letters"; by the fact that He was what we would call today a "man of letters."

It is always a revelation of disastrous failure when people are impressed more with what a man knows than with what a man is, or more with the college from which he was graduated than with his virtue.

In answer to their question how He knew so much Jesus answered them, and said: "My doctrine is not mine, but his that sent me" (John 7:16). In other words, His doctrine came from God.

Note that in answering them He referred to His teaching, not to His letters. The intelligentsia are interested only in letters; the intelligent are interested in teaching.

It was as if He said, Never mind my accent; get hold of my teaching — I am the Voice of God, and if you want to prove it, this is the way: "If any man will do the will of God, he shall know of the doctrine, whether it be of God, or whether I speak of myself" (John 7:17).

He placed the grasping of great intellectual truths in goodwill. This goodwill is in the masses, in those who work on our farms, in our industries, our delivery wagons, our stores, or who live on WPA relief. They might make fools of themselves on "Information Please," by not knowing the color of Henry VIII's beard, but their hearts are right, and their wills are strong.

What greater proof of it is needed than this fact: Communism is supposed to be the philosophy of life for the masses, their hope for an enlightened future, their vindicated justice, and their paradise on earth.

But despite its raucous appeal to what it calls the proletariat, the masses of America are untouched by Communist propaganda. They were not fooled, but the intelligentsia were. Communism has won more recruits in one single University in New York than it has won among all the farmhands of Illinois and Iowa put together.

The immigrant who works as an iron molder for $80.00 a month and supports five children is not duped by Communism; but the history professor who receives $300.00 a month of the taxpayers money and supports no children, is fooled, and fooled so badly one thinks of the line of Hamlet: "Let the doors be shut upon him; that he may play the fool nowhere but in his own house" — or should we say "in his own university"?

The worker being up against the economic facts of life sees better than the intelligentsia that Communism would work if it had someone to feed it and clothe it. But since the taxpayer feeds and clothes the professor, he thinks Communism would work.

The intelligentsia, like soldiers who shook their dice, would probably sit at the foot of the Cross of Christ, make an objective record of the execution, but never be impressed. They are either so proud they do not know their misery or, if they do know their misery, they do not know they need a redeemer.

But the masses, like the apostles, are susceptible to the spirit. The Cross offers them something unlike anything which the philosopher and the humanist preacher of "moral uplift" could offer them, and that is a firm foundation of life and thought.

The intelligentsia who talk of "self-expression" see only nonsense in the Cross; but the masses who feel a cross in the daily routine of their lives, know that only in someone crucified like themselves is there hope.

They want not a philosopher to tell them to rely on themselves and their fellowman alone; for they have been doing that all their lives. They look to someone who had to put his trust in God when a fellowman failed.

It is now as it was in the beginning. St. John tells us that when Our Lord went up to the Feast of the Tabernacles, and said, "If any man thirst, let him come to me, and drink" (John 7:37), the masses learning it, said: "This is the prophet indeed. ... This is the Christ" (John 7:40-41).

But the intelligentsia sent out orderlies to apprehend Him. The orderlies, being of the masses, were so impressed by Him they came back empty-handed.

The intelligentsia challenged: "Why have you not brought him?" and they answered, "Never did man speak like this man" (John 7:45-46).

What an amazing reason! They had heard Him utter those tremendous words,

challenging the thirst of humanity, and declaring that if men would believe in Him, out of their lives would flow blessings.
So they went back to the intelligentsia and said, in effect: "No, we did not arrest Him, He arrested us."

The intelligentsia thundered: "Are you also seduced?" (John 7:47). And then there came that singularly human retort so common today — they asked the orderlies if they knew anyone in the government or among the intelligentsia who believed in Him. It was a question of false pride and then a contempt for the masses who were so simple as to believe in the Divine, for "the multitude," they sneered, "are accursed." (John 7:49.)

Today they would say the masses are crazy, they are not; they are the beloved of God, they are the raw material which the truly intellectual must influence with their truths and sacrifices; they are the ones whom the Savior called Blessed; they are ours; He gave them to us.

The intelligentsia do not want them except as instruments of power, but we must want them as children of God and the hope of a better nation.

Your hands may be dirty with work, but your hearts are clean; you may not have the social columns on the occasion of a divorce, but your name is written in heaven as the husband of one wife or the wife of one husband, or a loyal and devoted friend to another aching heart.

You may keep dogs, but you keep them as companions of your children, not as substitutes for them; you may not have a college degree, but you know more than all the college professors scattered throughout the length and breadth of our land, who have not yet learned why they are here or where they are going.

You may be the tramp on the street, the old woman in the bread lines, the little child in the orphanage, but because you know God made you and act on that belief, you know more than Einstein — a thousand times more, for the man who knows how to get his head into the heavens is wiser than the scientist who knows only how to get the heavens into his head.

You know the secret of happiness, for since the world offered you so little, you looked for happiness not on the outside in material circumstances, but on the inside —for "the kingdom of God is within you" (Luke 17:21).

You may commit sin, but you admit it and put the blame on your will, not on bad glands or visceral rumblings; and hence you make your redemption possible. You are not the radicals nor the subversive elements in this country — radicalism, and want of patriotism come not from below but from above.

Where among religious groups do you find the greatest degree of theological and social radicalism, if it be not among the affluent suburban churches? It is they who told you Christ was not God; it is they who told you divorce is right, and it is they who, choosing among barbarities, taught you to despise Fascism —but not Communism with it.

It was from among you common people the Savior of the world chose His Apostles; it was among you He labored as a carpenter; it was principally from among you the Church recruited her apostles and her saints, and it is among you now that the Church looks for the salt that will renovate the earth when a false wisdom without God finishes its destructive hour.

It is your virtues — the virtues of the common man the world needs now, not the sophistries of the intelligentsia; it is even your pleasures — the pleasures of the common man we need to restore us to sanity — not the excitement of intellectual slummers.

The days of the Superman are about over; he is dying on the battlefields of Europe. The hour of the common man is dawning, for though the intelligentsia call you ignorant, your ignorance has all the exquisite intuitions of innocence; it is the kind of foolishness which St. Paul says God calls wise.

For when the self-wise enthroned Jesus on the Cross and then blasphemed and ridiculed, it was one of the masses, a common soldier, who stepped forward and said: "Indeed this was the Son of God" (Matt. 27:54).

That is the kind of vision we need now, for the men and women who see that truth will save the world when the politicians and economists fail.

But what shall the educated do, the truly wise, the intellectuals — not the intelligentsia? They shall serve you.

And may not anyone among them feel it is beneath his dignity, for shall he forget that the Teacher who is the Wisdom of God Itself, came to this earth teaching little children and fishermen?

LIBERAL AND REACTIONARY

The two most abused and thoughtlessly used words in our day are "Liberal" and "Reactionary."

These epithets come into prominence whenever wars, revolutions, or depressions disturb an established order. They are born of rapid changes in the tempo of political, economic, or social life.

Now change implies two elements: First, something which changes and, second, something which does not change; in other words something movable and something immutable.

For example, when meeting a friend whom you have not seen for twenty years, you say, "How you have changed." If this person were not the same person now as twenty years ago, you would not know he had changed. In other words, you cannot recognize change without the changeless.

The reactionary and the liberal have this in common: They never see permanence and change together. They take one to the exclusion of the other. The reactionary seizes upon permanency to the exclusion of change, and the liberal upon change to the exclusion of permanency.

Both are extremists, and because they are extremists both are wrong.

The reactionary wants things to remain as they are; the liberal wants change though he is little concerned with its direction.

The word liberal is derived from "liber" the ancient god of wine, and hence the term originally and obviously implied intoxication. Shakespeare evidently had that in mind when he wrote in Henry VIII, "When you are a liberal, be sure you are not loose."

The reactionary has rather correctly been defined as a man who has two feet and new shoes, but does not know how to walk, and a liberal as one who has both feet firmly planted in mid-air.

The reactionary believes that change in the present order is revolution; the liberal believes that change demands the repudiation of sacred and inviolable principles.

The reactionary says: "Johnnie wears a green hat now; Johnnie will wear a green hat in the summer, spring, autumn, and winter;

when he is fourteen and when he is forty; he will wear it to breakfast, dinner, and supper." The liberal says: "No, style and conditions have so changed, give Johnnie a new head."

The reactionary wants the clock, but no time; the liberal wants the time, but no clock. The reactionary believes in staying where he is, though he never inquires whether or not he has a right to be there; the liberal, on the contrary, never knows where he is going, he is only sure he is on his way.

The reactionary, instead of working towards an ideal, stagnates; while the liberal instead of working towards an ideal, changes the ideal and calls it progress.

There is a golden mean between the reactionary and the liberal, and the word that seems to fit best is 'Catholic.' It avoids the reactionary position which would make Johnnie always wear a green hat, and the liberal position which would give Johnnie a new head, by letting Johnnie keep his head but giving him a new hat. It admits change without sacrificing the permanent and valuable.

Because a social order needs changing, the Catholic no more advocates the scrapping of the abiding principles of traditional morality than he advocates cutting an arm to fit a sleeve. Just as the cells in a human body change about every seven years and yet man remains identically the same person at seventy that he was at seven, so too, the Church contends, one can reconcile permanence with change without choosing permanence without change, or change without permanence.

The Catholic position can best be described in the scene of its foundation. One day our Blessed Lord entered into that ancient City of Caesarea Philippi, where He asked the most important question in the world: "Whom do men say that I am?"

When men gave contradictory answers and the apostles gave none, one man, Peter, speaking in the name of all and with Divine illumination, answered: "Thou art Christ, the son of the Living God."

In answer to this, the Divine Savior made Peter, as his name implied, the rock of His Church, and gave him the power of keys: "Thou art Peter; and upon this rock I will build my Church, and the gates of hell shall not prevail against it. And I will give to thee the keys of the kingdom of heaven." (Matt. 16:8, 19.)

In founding His Church Our Lord combined two elements: The immutable and the mutable, the permanent and the changing.

The Church would be immutable in her Truth — no other doctrine would ever be given it, not even by the angels; not a single iota of it would ever be changed; it would be as immutable as Divinity, as intolerant as the multiplication table, as absolute as its Giver.

But that truth would need to be applied to different times and different circumstances. Since it was to last unto the consummation of the world, it would need a different emphasis for the twelfth century than for the first, and a different one for the twentieth than for the sixteenth. There would have to be something mutable in that immutable edifice.

The immutable, changeless character was signified by the Rock; the mutable, changing character was signified by the keys. Truth, morality, and justice would be unshakable like the Rock enduring to the crack of doom; but the truth, morality, and justice would have to be applied to different social, economic, and political conditions, for the civilization of the fifth century would not be the same as the thirteenth, nor the thirteenth the same as the nineteenth.

Hence, Our Lord said, in effect, to Peter: For what is right and good in social and economic order you may open the door, but for what is wrong and false you close the door. Hence, I give you the power of keys: "Whatsoever thou shalt bind upon earth it shall be bound also in heaven, and whatsoever thou shalt loose upon earth, it shall be loosed also in heaven" (Matt. 16:19).

This use of the words rock and key by Our Divine Lord gives the answer to that group of so-called Liberal writers who recently proclaimed: "The absoluteness of the Church is inconsistent with the relativity of history" (City of Man — page 40). This is just like saying the absoluteness of the multiplication table is inconsistent with the relatives of history, for now, we no longer count pyramids but skyscrapers.

A Catholic is neither a reactionary nor a liberal in the sense of the terms above defined. He is not a reactionary because the Catholic knows that if you leave things alone you will not leave them as they are.

If you leave a cornfield alone, you do not have corn but weeds; if you leave a white fence alone, you soon have a black fence.

So too the Catholic says: If you leave man alone without vigilance and discipline, you have either a rusted man or a rotted man, for man decays more rapidly than he evolves, as modern history so well demonstrates.

Neither will the Catholic be a liberal who wants to make progress by scrapping eternal principles and ideals. The Catholic argues that unless you have a fixed point of departure and a fixed goal, you never know you are making any progress.

How can an artist know he is making progress in painting if every time he looks up from the canvas he finds a different person sitting for his portrait?

The terms reactionary and liberal are so relative they mean little to thinking men who have either a knowledge of history or a remnant of reason.

For example, the liberal of the last generation invoked liberalism to free economic activity from state control; the liberal of today invokes liberalism to extend state control over the economic order.

The old liberal was a defender of Capitalism; the new liberal is reacting against

Capitalism and wants some form of collectivism or state control.

The old liberal wanted liberty of press, speech, and conscience within the framework of democracy; the new liberal, reacting against the old liberalism, wants the liberty without the framework as its safeguard.

The old liberal rebelled against taxation without responsibility; the new liberal wants the taxation as a handout without responsibility.

The old liberal fifty years ago was materialistic in science. His son who calls himself a liberal is today's reactionary for whom science is idealistic.

The French Liberals who protested against the authority of King and Altar in the name of Liberty, were reactionaries, for they did not believe in extending that liberty to the proletariat.

Many liberals who wrote they believed in the equality of all men, kept slaves. To change it around, every reactionary is protesting against the last liberal.

Sometimes in one man the liberal and the reactionary meet, as they did in the case of Milton.

Milton was a liberal who favored a free press and protested against licensing of books; and then when a handsome salary was offered him he reacted against his liberalism and became an official censor of books.
All that we have in the world is reaction against reactions; revolt against revolts; the reactionary and liberal are on a see-saw, and think they are going places because they are going up and down and see their momentary triumph over their opponent.

In the strict sense of the term, there are no liberals. A liberal is only a reactionary, reacting against the last form of liberalism.

The new liberals are at war against the old liberals; the new rebels in rebellion against the old rebels. The liberal of today will be the reactionary of tomorrow.

This simple analogy will help to make clear how our so-called liberalism is only a reaction against the last liberalism.

A woman buys a new dress for a ball to be held, say on the first of May. This dress is the last word in style; in political language it is "liberal,' 'progressive,' far ahead of the reactionaries who bought their dresses last year.

At the ball, jealous and envious eyes are cast upon her, and to her face, the most flattering of compliments. Even the word "daring" is used.

Now it happens that she is invited to another ball, one month later and with the same group of people, and in the same place. Would that woman wear the same gown? She would not. She would rather die first!

Why would she not wear it? Because people had seen it before. She would no longer be liberal. She must have a new gown for the new ball.

In order to be a liberal in June, she has to be a reactionary against her liberal gown of May. That is why I say every liberal is reactionary.

The Church believes it is possible to make a distinction between being fashionable and being well dressed.

Consider, for example, the vestments worn by the priest at the altar. They certainly are not fashionable, for they are really an adaptation of the old Roman toga; but though you never see a chasuble in a fashion magazine, who would deny that the priest at the altar is becomingly and beautifully clothed.

The ideas of the Church are like her vestments; always well dressed but never the slave of passing fashion.

The Church knows after 1900 years' experience that any institution which suits the spirit of any age will be a widow in the next one. The Church, therefore, will never please either the reactionary or the liberal.

She will please only the relatively few who can understand how a house built on an immutable rock with an abiding proprietor, Peter, has a key that admits strangers.

The reactionaries want the rock without the keys; the liberals want the keys without the rock; and we who believe in Christ, who gave both to Peter, want both.

You have been told that the only choice possible is to be a reactionary or a liberal; that you must go either right or left. That would be true if you lived on a two-dimensional plane and this world were all; but you have a soul as well as a body.

You need therefore a three-dimensional universe, one with height where you can stretch not your legs but your hearts.

A mule can travel only in two directions; either right or left. He must be either a reactionary or a liberal. But because you have a soul there is another direction open to you, namely toward God for whom you were made.

Let the unthinking squabble about what a grandson ought to believe, or what a grandfather did believe, but concentrate on what a godson believes because born of the Spirit.

If you are honest with yourself you will admit that you are wary of religions, politics, and panaceas that flatter the way you live; you want something that will contradict the way you live and therefore be capable of redeeming you; you are sick of revolutions that only change booty and loot from one man's pocket into another's; you want a revolution that will change your hearts.

Leave it to the comedians to talk about "progress" when humanity is preying upon itself, for what they call progress is only a process — the fashion of the world passing away.

You are weary of the see-saw of reactionaries and liberals; you want a force and a spiritual power that will be hated by both, as Our Divine Lord was hated and considered a menace by the reactionary Pharisees and a disturbing factor by the liberal Herodians.

You want today a force that will rescue you from the evil in the world and still let you do good in the world; which unlike the world will not tell you to go right or left, but up: "And I, if I be lifted up from the earth, will draw all things to myself" (John 12:32).

That is what you want: I do not know whether you have found it. Would it interest you to know that I have?

I have found it in the heart of Christendom, in the crystallization of common sense, in the living memory of the centuries, in the Church built upon a Rock and governed by the Man with Keys.

I have found it in that which is hated as much as Christ was hated, misunderstood, and maligned as much as He was maligned, but loved as much as He was loved.

I have found it in an institution which millions who are not of its fold recognize as

the only moral authority left in the world. I
find it in the Church which is prolonged
Christ, whom the reactionaries find too liberal
and the liberals too reactionary; something
that challenges the world not pampers it;
which speaks a truth that because it is God-
made, cannot be man-remade; which restores
me to the Savior's embrace when I sin; which
nourishes my soul with the life of Christ when
I hunger; which leads me to Calvary when I
become undisciplined; which thrusts before
me a Cross to inspire service of sacrifice for
the poor; which tells me what is right when
the world is wrong; and which will minister to
my soul when my lease on life is ended. In a
word, I am neither a Reactionary nor a Liberal
— Civis Romanus sum! I am a Catholic!

THE FOUR COLUMNS

America has no need of stressing a danger from without — our press, cinema, radio, and government are of one voice in warning us against dictators.

But it is the duty of those interested in God and morality and peace to emphasize a less popular theme — and a more needed one — the danger from within.

There is no reason why America with its tremendous natural and technical resources should be overcome from the outside; but very frankly, our greatest danger is from the inside.

Our present temper is to assume that our hatred for sixty-six and two-thirds percent of cruel dictators can provide the discipline, order and authority essential for the preservation of a nation.

It is the purpose of this chapter to challenge that mood and to suggest that a strengthening of our moral fibre must go hand in hand with military preparedness that we be seized from within.

History, Scripture, and nature all come to us freighted with a warning that the graver danger facing individuals and nations is from within rather than from without.

A distinguished historian of London, Professor Toynbee, proves that out of nineteen civilizations in the history of the world no less than sixteen broke down through their own acts before any alien human force succeeded in dealing them a mortal blow.

In sixteen out of nineteen cases all that the foreign enemy did was to give the last blow to a civilization that had already committed suicide; or to change the figure, to devour the carcass after it had already become carrion.

The collapses of these civilizations have not been due to circumstances beyond their control; they were neither the inexorable verdicts of cruel Fate, nor the prey of sadistic sport of barbarious warriors, nor the result of catastrophes like floods, fires, and shipwrecks; nor were they the effect of an assassin's blow.

In practically sixteen out of nineteen cases, the historian, as the coroner of civilization, wrote down the verdict of "suicide."

In rebuking the Pharisees who were over-concerned with externals, Our Divine Lord said that the things that come into a man from the outside do not defile him, "but the things which proceed out of the mouth, come forth from the heart, and those things defile a man. For from the heart come forth evil thoughts, murders, adulteries, fornications, thefts, false testimonies, blasphemies. These are the things that defile a man." (Matt. 15, 19-20.)

And we might add that since they defile a man they must also defile a nation. Defeat springs less from invasion than from corruption.

Shall we as a whole nation be so self-righteous as to become indignant against applying to ourselves the warning to the Pharisees: "Thou blind Pharisee, first make clean the inside of the cup and of the dish that the outside may become clean. Woe to you ... you are like to whitened sepulchres, which outwardly appear to men beautiful, but within are full of dead men's bones." (Matt. 23:26, 27.)

If we turn from God to the nature He made we find the same warning. Collect a flock of pigeons of every shade, color, and marking, then take them to an uninhabited island, and after many years all the pigeons will be one color — a dark slaty blue.

Neglect keeping a garden in order and it will run to weeds; neglect your muscles and they stiffen.

Human life is not always surging upwards by evolution as our pseudo-scientists told us, it is also tumbling downwards by devolution.

Human nature is not only subject to conversion; it may even be subject to reversion and perversion.

Degeneration is a fact of life to which we have been blinded by loose talk about progress; it is now time to face the bias of evil; the possibility of gravitation by which a man gathering momentum as he falls further from God, lands in the hell of a neglected and ruined life.

The tragedy of life is that this ruin may be so gradual and imperceptible that while concentrating on external dangers the citadel of life is taken from within.

As the poet Meredith put it:

"In tragic life, God wot
No villain need be! Passions spin the plot;
We are betrayed by what is false within."

And as the old Greek poet Meander put it so long ago:

"Things rot through evils native to themselves And all that injures issues from within."

And by false within I mean not the Fifth Columnists, because a Fifth Columnist could not operate if there were not already four other columnists. The breakdown of civilization is due more to an inward loss of self-determination than to external blows.

Take for example, the formation of rust on a bar of iron. When the iron begins to disintegrate, there is a dislocation of some of its molecules, which permits the infiltration of an alien force from the outside, namely, the free oxygen in the air. The union of the two produces rust.

The Fifth Columnists correspond to the oxygen in the air; they are the alien social forces. But these Fifth Columnists could never become a part of a civilization unless a decay had already set in within the nation itself.

Iron can be kept from rusting; civilization can be kept from degenerating. But neglect makes rust and decay possible. If we had not abandoned Absolute Truth; if we had not adopted the stupid moral philosophy that freedom means the right to do whatever you please, even the right to destroy freedom, we would have no Fifth Columnists.

That is why I say the Fifth Columnist is possible only because there are already Fourth Columnists and these constitute our danger from within. What are these four Columns?

The First Columnists are those educators and publicists who reject a universal norm of morality in favor of a relative morality based either on expediency, pleasure, profit or selfishness of the individual; in other words, a rejection of the principle that right is right if nobody is right and wrong is wrong if everybody is wrong.

A typical instance of this abandonment of morality based on God and His justice is the tendency in international relations to call Russia a "friendly nation" when the facts prove that Russia has been just as destructive of humanity, as hateful of religion, as oppressive of the masses and as cruel to hearts as the Nazis — and that is as damning an indictment as could be made of any nation.

We Americans may not say and we must not say before God that we are fighting for freedom of speech, freedom of religion, and freedom from fear, when we choose among the barbarians and dictators and call that nation "friendly" which gave the green light to Hitler to invade the West, and which within its own boundaries as prison walls has extinguished the rights and liberties of 160,000,000 people.

The First Column undermines justice, the Second Column undermines charity. The Second Columnists are those who sin against charity and include all those who sin not only by rejecting the solidarity of mankind, because begotten of a common origin and redeemed by Our Divine Lord, but also by rebelling against the fraternal spirit and tolerance which should exist between citizens of the same country.

In this Second Column are those in the ranks of Capital and Labor who through avarice on the one hand and envy and greed on the other turn the nation into a warring camp at the very moment we talk about a war from the outside.

In this Second Column, too, are those individuals who are guilty of anti-Semitism, anti-Catholicism, bigotry, atheism, and immorality, who by their hatreds are not murdering bodies but slaughtering souls with eternal destinies and for which they will one day have to answer before the Judgment Seat of Almighty God.

The Third Columnists are those lawyers, jurists, and teachers who by divorcing civil authority from dependence on the Law of God, make law only an instrument for action, or the social expression of the way beings live, rather than the way they ought to live.

In this Third Column are those so-called educators who complain against the release time from school for religious instruction in the nonsensical plea that it means the union of Church and State.

It is interesting to note that the persons who most oppose religion for the young as being un-American, are often the same ones who draw money from American tax-payers to tie us up with anti-American activities.

Let me say to these Third Columnists that there is no danger in this country of the union of the Church and State, but there is danger of the union of atheism and the State.

If that is what they want, then let them say so, and we will fight back in the name of the Declaration of Independence — Washington, and Lincoln — in a word, in the name of America.

The Fourth Columnists are those who either explicitly or implicitly adhere to the philosophy of "self-expression" and reject the necessity of discipline, authority, and self-sacrifice as the condition of individual and national betterment.

In this Fourth Column are those who think they should get everything for nothing in America and still have the right to complain about the quality; those who refuse to face the responsibility of spending and thus mortgage America's future; those who consider education a social necessity rather than an intellectual privilege; those labor leaders and those Capitalists who shout "Persecution" as soon as one of their own is convicted of injustice by the government; those parents who are raising a bumper crop of spoiled children because they see too many exhibitions and learn too few inhibitions; those who sue the school and the Board of Education if a teacher scolds for an act of wrongdoing their "darling child" who can do no wrong; and finally those who pamper the rapacious egotism of their children and thus prevent the formation of good habits.

Given amalgamation in iron, you will get rust by the moisture from outside, given these four columns in the inside of a nation, you get the alien Fifth Columnists boring from within.

St. Cyprian centuries ago saw that something had gone wrong with the internal economy of Hellenic civilization; something had crept into the hearts of people which made then so sick on the inside that he wanted to save them.

"You complain of the aggression of foreign enemies; yet, if the foreign enemy were to cease from troubling, would Roman really be able to live at peace with Roman (esse pax inter ipsas togas possit?).

"If the external danger of invasion by armed barbarians were to be stamped out, should we: not be exposed to a fiercer and a heavier civil bombardment on the home front, in the shape of calumnies and injuries inflicted by the powerful upon their weaker fellow citizens?

"You complain of crop failures and famine; yet the greatest famines are made not by drought but by rapacity, and the most flagrant distress springs from profiteering and price raising in the corn trade.

"You complain that the clouds do not disgorge their rain in the sky, and you ignore the barns that fail to disgorge their grain on terra firma. You complain of the fall in production, and ignore the failure to distribute

90

what is actually produced to those who are in need of it.

"You denounce plague and pestilence, while really the effect of these scourges is to bring to light, or bring to a head, the crimes of human beings: the callousness that shows no pity for the sick, and the covetousness and rapine that are in full cry after the property of the dead." (Thascius Caecilius Cyprianus: Ad Demetrianum-Chapter 10.)

All can be summed up in a word, we need a little more self-discipline, in the form of less selfishness, less hate, less avarice, more sacrifice, more tolerance, more respect for law and authority, more morality, more God.

This much is certain: We will have discipline in the future, and if we do not enforce it freely upon ourselves, we will have it imposed from without — a cruel, tyrannical discipline.

Want of discipline and morality brought on the slave states of Russia in 1918, Germany in 1933, and the totalitarian state of Italy in 1922, and the fallen France of 1940. All these people disintegrated from within before they disintegrated from without.

Every totalitarian state has arisen out of confusion, humiliation, frustration; having no order they were willing to try anything.

Let not America be blind to history, to revelation and to nature and talk only of the enemy from without and not of the enemy from within, or concentrate on Fifth Columnists and forget the other four. This rebirth of national discipline will not be easy to achieve.

It is unfortunately true that totalitarian states can more readily appeal to sacrifice than some democracies, for having imbued their people with a diabolical mysticism and having infused them with a false fervor, they are ready to deny themselves for a future glory.

But when democracies lose the spirit of religion they have no fulcrum for self-sacrifice; once the Cross passes out of their vision selfishness enthrones itself. Then the plea for self-sacrifice becomes identified with persecution, Fascism, Communism, or what-have-you.

The preservation of America is conditioned upon discipline and self-sacrifice, but since these are inseparable from religion and morality, the future of America depends on

Americans' attitude toward God and the Cross of His Divine Son.

Is not a call to penance and self-sacrifice within the tradition of America? Has not our country before always in times of crisis called upon its citizens not only to pray, but to do penance, to fast, to humiliate themselves before God, and to make themselves worthy instruments of His Justice?

Shall we in America forget that John Adams in 1799 proclaimed that "in circumstances of great urgency and seasons of imminent danger earnest and particular supplications should be made to God Who is able to defend or to destroy"?

Have we forgotten that when this new and weak nation was swept into the Napoleonic Wars, that President Madison, three times between 1812 and 1815, called for "public humiliation for the transgressions which might justly provoke the manifestations of His Divine Displeasure?"

Have we as Americans forgotten in the trying days of civil strife President Buchanan set aside January 4, 1861, as the day when "all people should assemble according to their several forms of worship, to keep a solemn fast?"

Have we forgotten that five times during his Presidency, Abraham Lincoln called on the people to "bow down in humble submission to God's chastisement to confess and deplore their sins and transgressions in the full conviction that the fear of the Lord is the beginning of wisdom, and to pray with all fervency and contrition for the pardon of past offenses, that we might be spared further punishment, though most justly deserved and that the Throne of Love might bring down plentiful blessings on our country?"

Have we forgotten that moving plea of Andrew Jackson for a day of humbling ourselves before Almighty God?"

Do we remember that Grant in 1871 set aside November 30 as a day for asking Almighty God for "merciful exemptions from evils?"

Have we forgotten that the last Presidential Proclamation issued in the United States which admitted the possibility that we ought to ask God for something else than prosperity and which envisaged the possibility that we needed some regeneration was that of President Wilson who proclaimed Thursday, May 30, 1918, as a day of "public humiliation, prayer and fasting?"

Do we remember that one day when the Apostles came to Our Lord they confessed their inability to drive out certain devils? Our Lord told them that kind was driven out only by prayers and fasting.

That is the only way the devils of the modern world can be driven out, not only by prayers but by fasting, by sacrifice, by self-discipline.

And if ever our President in keeping with the traditions of America should ask not only for prayers for prosperity, but for humiliation, fasting for our sins, and a renewed spirit of discipline for the sake of America under God, then let us respond, strengthening our moral fibre; for America will never be beaten from without, as long as it is moral from within.

THE CROSS AND
THE DOUBLE-CROSS

The Cross is not incredible to the modern mind, for nothing is more understandable than sacrificial love; rather it is irrelevant.

A person who denies there is such a thing as sickness does not consider the physician a myth; he considers him irrelevant. In like manner, if one denies he is a sinner how can he need redemption?

The sense of guilt, as we have been emphasizing throughout this book, is considered today only as a vestigial remnant of primitive fears, or as a "psychopathic aspect of an adolescent mentality."

If there is guilt in the world, it lies in systems, not in persons — such is the modern mentality.

In the 18th century this sort of mind attributed evil to tyrannical governments; in the 19th century to tyrannical classes; and in the 20th century to dictatorships — not all dictatorships of course, only two-thirds of them; for Russia, it is said is a "friendly nation." Yes! Friendly like Judas who blistered the lips of Christ with a kiss.

Since nothing can disturb the modern man's good opinion of himself, the Cross with its Redemption is meaningless. But it is not as irrelevant as he thinks.

The purpose of this chapter is to indicate that by denying the Cross of Christ, modern man did not escape a cross — no one can; he got a cross — the double-cross.

What happened to the Prodigal Son in the Gospel happened to the modern man. In the first scene he threw off the yoke of the Father's house to live his own life; or, in the language of our day, to be "self-expressive" and "free," independent of all restraints.

In the second scene, his wealth is gone, his stomach empty, his heart heavy. But do we find him free and independent?

On the contrary he becomes a slave to the citizen of a foreign country feeding his swine, whose husks he would have eaten to have filled his belly — no longer his heart — but no man gave him to eat. He who wanted to be free found himself a slave.

Something like that has happened to the modern man. For the last 400 years he has been striving for total independence and absolute autonomy: First from the Church as a spiritual organism; then from the Bible as the revealed word of God; then from the authority of Christ; and finally from religion.

By progressive steps he rebelled against his Divine destiny. Like the steward who pretended to be the master of the vineyard, he killed his lord's messenger, that he might possess it forever. Like the prodigal he squandered his spiritual capital until he had nothing to eat except the husks of humanism and behaviorism.

He made himself a god, and, in the language of teachers of philosophy in dozens of American universities, he called himself "a creator rather than a creature."

Because man was a god, it followed he could do no wrong. Since he could not sin, he needed no Calvary. The Cross he hated — as George Bernard Shaw, spokesman for the modern man, said: "The Cross in the twilight bars the way.

So modern man forged an educational system without discipline; he fashioned a philosophy which denied truth, and made good and evil only relative to the individual; he labeled every attempt to restore authority as "Fascism"; every restriction on the part of the government against economic selfishness as "Communism"; and every arrest of racketeers and Communist labor leaders as "Nazi persecution."

He formed civil liberty associations to defend every attempt to destroy civil liberty; and, as a sop to sentimentalism, he made a religion without Hell, a Christ without Justice, a Kingdom of God without God, salvation without a Crucifix, and a Church where a pulpit and an organ replaced the altar of sacrifice.

In a word, he refused to see the connection between his own selfish autonomy and the chaos which that selfish autonomy produced in others, and which he hated in them.

He was not as logical as Nietzsche who saw that man must either accept the Cross or go mad — and Nietzsche went mad.

Now we are at scene two. As the prodigal found there was no escaping some kind of submission, so the modern man learned that there is no such thing as escaping the Cross. Absolute independence is a myth.

Man is truly free only when he acts within the law and not outside it or against it, I am free to draw a triangle only on condition that I give it three sides and not, in a stroke of progressive broadmindedness, thirty-three.

I am free to fly in a plane only on condition that I submit myself to the laws of gravitation. To want to be free from that law is not to be free to fly, but to be free to fall. The penalty for the violation of law is unfreedom or slavery.

Sin is the opposite of freedom. For that reason Our Lord said, "whosoever committeth sin, is the servant of sin" (John 8:34).

If a man gives himself over to drink he loses his freedom; he becomes the servant or the slave of sin.

He began by being free to take a drink or not to take a drink; he ended by being no longer free to do anything but take it.

To be a slave of passion is the opposite of freedom. In seeking to be absolutely independent of God and morality, man lost his freedom.

Freedom, as absolute independence, is impossible. Our liberals who wanted a freedom without authority found that out.

The choice is not: Will we or will we not accept authority? It is rather: Which authority will we accept, the authority of Christ or the authority of public opinion.

Those who rejected Divine Truth did not become free-minds; they became slave-minds. That is why so many of them cannot make a judgment about anything until they read the Gallup poll or the morning newspaper.

Furthermore, there is no such thing as freedom from discipline. We may only choose between disciplines: A discipline from the inside freely administered by our own sense of righteous, self-perfection, or a discipline from the outside inspired by cruel, tyrannical forces.

And that brings us to the point we want to prove: That there is no such thing as living without a cross.

We are free only to choose between crosses. Will it be the Cross of Christ which redeems us from our sins, or will it be the Double-Cross, the Swastika, the hammer and sickle, the fasces?

Why are we a troubled nation today? Why do we live in fear — we who defined freedom as the right to do whatever we pleased; we who have no altars in our churches, no discipline in our schools, and no sacrifices in our lives? We fear because our false freedom and license and apostasy from God has caught up with us, as it did with the Prodigal.

We would not accept the yoke of Christ; so now we must tremble at the yoke of Caesar. We willed to be free from God; now we must face the danger of being enslaved to a citizen of a foreign country.

In seeking to live without the Cross, we got a cross — not one of Christ's making or our own, but the devil's! — a diabolically cruel, tortured cross made of guns, hammers, sickles, and bombs — the thing that started out to be a cross and then double-crossed itself because it has double-crossed the world.

And that threat throws us into a terrific dilemma. Can we meet that double-cross without the Cross?

Can a democracy of ease and comfort overcome a system built on sacrifice? Can a nation which permits the break-up of the family by divorce, defeat a nation which forcefully bends the family to the nation? Can they, who for seven years tightened their belts, gave up butter for guns, endured every conceivable limitation, be conquered by ease and comfort?

Dr. Alexis Carrel was right in saying that in America: "A good time has been our national cry. The perfect life as viewed by the average youth or adult is a round of ease or entertainment; of motion pictures, radio programs, parties, alcohol, and sexual excesses. This indolent and undisciplined way of life has sapped our individual vigor and imperiled our democratic form of government. Our race pitifully needs new supplies of discipline, morality, and intelligence."

The rise of Militarism and the Gospel of Force in the modern world is a result of the vacuum created by the abandonment of the Cross.

Europe was nourished on Christian virtues; it knew obedience to authority, self-discipline, penance, and the need of redemption. But when it began to starve through the abandonment of the Bread of the Father's House, it seized, like the Prodigal, on the fodder of militarism and the glorification of the sword.

Like the empty house of the Gospel, the modern world swept itself clean of the Cross of

Christ, but only to be possessed by the devils of the double-cross.

As Voltaire said: "If man had no God, he would make himself one!" So too, we might add, if man had no Cross, he would make himself one. And he has.

Apostate from Calvary, the glorification of military virtues in these states is the feeble compensation for a yoke that is sweet and a burden that is light.

As Mussolini said on August 24, 1934, "We are becoming a warlike nation — that is to say, one endowed to a higher degree with virtues of obedience, sacrifice, and dedication to country."

This so-called heroic attitude toward life is being invoked in deadly earnest by millions in Germany and Russia, and by all who espouse their cause in other nations.

In the days when the Cross lived in the hearts of men, war was considered a calamity, a scourge sent by God; but now in the days of the double-cross, it is justified as the noblest of virtues for the sake of the nation as in Italy, the race as in Germany, and the class as in Russia.

They believe what Von Moltke wrote in 1880: "Without War the world would become swamped in materialism." Imagine! To save us from materialism, we must have war!

He is right in saying that to save us from materialism we must have sacrifice. He is wrong in saying it must come from war. But if there is no Cross to inspire it, whence shall it come but from the double-cross?

We in America are now faced with the threat of that double-cross. To revert to our theme. Our choice is not: Will we or will we not have more discipline, more respect for law, more order, more sacrifice; but, where will we get it?

Will we get it from without, or from within? Will it be inspired by Sparta or Calvary? By Valhalla or Gethsemane? By Militarism or Religion? By the double-cross or the Cross? By Caesar or by God?

That is the choice facing America today. The hour of false freedom is past. No longer can we have education without discipline, family life without sacrifice, individual existence without moral responsibility, economics and politics without subservience to the common good. We are now only free to say whence it shall come.

We will have a sword. Shall it be only the sword that thrusts outward to cut off the ears of our enemies, or the sword that pierces inward to cut out our own selfish pride?

May heaven grant that, unlike the centurion, we pierce not the heart of Christ before we discover His Divinity and Salvation.

Away with those educators and propagandists who, by telling us we need no Cross, make possible having one forged for us abroad. Away with those who, as we gird ourselves for sacrifice based on love of God and Calvary, sneer: "Come down from the Cross" (Matt. 27:40).

That cry has been uttered before on Calvary, as His enemies shouted: "He saved others, himself he cannot save" (Mark 15:31).

They were now willing to admit he had saved others; they could well afford to do it for now He apparently could not save Himself.

Of course, He could not save Himself. No man can save himself who saves another.

The rain cannot save itself, if it is to bud the greenery; the sun cannot save itself if it is to light the world; the seed cannot save itself if it is to make the harvest; a mother cannot save herself if she is to save her child; a soldier cannot save himself if he is to save his country.

It was not weakness which made Christ hang on the Cross; it was obedience to the law of sacrifice, of love. For how could He save us if He ever saved Himself?

Peace He craved; but as St. Paul says: "There is no peace but through the blood of the Cross." Peace we want; but there is none apart from sacrifice.

Peace is not a passive, but an active virtue. Our Lord never said: "Blessed are the peaceful," but "Blessed are the Peacemakers." The Beatitude rests only on those who make it out of trial, out of suffering, out of cruelty, even out of sin.

God hates peace in those who are destined for war. And we are destined for war — a war against a false freedom which endangered our freedom; a war for the Cross against the double-cross; a war to make America once more what it was intended to be from the beginning — a country dedicated to liberty under God; a war of the militia Christi: "Having our loins girt about with truth and having on the breastplate of justice ... the shield of faith ... the helmet of salvation (Eph. 6:10-17).

Only those who carry the Sword of the Spirit have the right and have the power to say to the enemies of the Cross, "Put thy sword back into its scabbard."

The great tragedy is that the torch of sacrifice and truth has been snatched from the hands of those who should hold it, and is borne aloft by the enemies of the Cross.

The Pentecostal fires have been stolen from the altar of God and now burn as tongues of fire in those who grind the altars into dust.

The fearlessness born of love of God which once challenged the armies of Caesar is now espoused to Caesar.

We live in an age of saints in reverse, when apostles who are breathed on by the evil spirit outdare those animated by the Holy Spirit of God.

The fires for causes like Communism, Nazism, and Fascism, that burn downwards, are more intense than the fires that burn upwards in the hearts of those who pay only lip service to God.

But this passion by which men deliver themselves over to half-truths and idiocies should make us realize what a force would enter history again if there were but a few saints in every nation who could help the world, because they were not enmeshed in it; who would, like their Master on the Cross, not seek to save the world as it is, but to be saved from it; who would demonstrate to those who still have decent hearts, as we believe we have in America, that it is possible to practice sacrifice without turning the world into a vast slaughterhouse.

There is no escaping the Cross!

That is why the hope, the real hope of the world, is not in those politicians who, indifferent to Divinity, offer Christ and Barabbas to the mob to save their tumbling suffrage.

It is not in those economists who would drive Christ from their shores like the Gerasens, because they feared loss of profit on their swine.

It is not in those educators who, like other Pilates, sneer: "What is Truth" — then Crucify it.

The hope of the world is in the crucified in every land in those bearing the Cross of Christ; in the mothers of Poland who, like other Rachels, mourn for their children; in the wives weeping for their husbands stolen into the servitude of war; in the sons and daughters kissing the cold earth of Siberia as the only one of the things God made that they are left to see; in bleeding feet and toil-worn hands; in persecuted Jews, blood-brothers of Christ, of whom God said: "He who curses you, I shall curse"; in the priests in concentration camps who, like Christ, in other Gethsemanes, find a way to offer their own blood in the chalice of their own body.

The hope of the world is in the Cross of Christ borne down the ages in the hearts of suffering men, women, and children, who, if we only knew it are saving us from the double-cross more than our guns and ships.

We in America are now brought face to face with the heritage of a freedom derived from God. The hour has struck when we have to take up a Cross. There is no escaping the Cross.

Who shall give it to us? Shall it be imposed by chastisement, or shall it be freely accepted by penance?

Let us believe in America's power of regeneration. Let us believe we can remake ourselves from within in order that we be not remade from without. Let us believe in the future of America; but let us believe in it only as we believe in Easter— after it has passed through Good Friday.

HOPE

We live in one of those interludes of history that come upon us once every few hundred years. It is a time between times, the end of one era and the beginning of another which is yet clouded in mist, that twilight zone when darkness seems so real and the light seems so far away.

The whole world seems to be possessed of a sense of impending catastrophe, when liberals doubt their own liberalism, reactionaries fear their own immobility; when defeat, persecution of religion, frustration of hearts, the enthronement of violence, and a gnawing fear, turn the prophets of progress into prophets of despair.

As the Jews of old sometimes yearned for the flesh-pots of Egypt, so does the modern man look back regretfully at what he thought was a paradise on earth, when poets sang "glory to man in the highest," when evolution promised to make each of us gods, and philosophers taught man was the measure of all things, when novelists pictured a "Brave New World," when education, politics, and economics no longer needed religion, and when the laws of progress guaranteed us a world without a Cross.

No period in history better reflects the pessimism and despair of our day than that tragic interlude between Good Friday and Easter Sunday, when the Light was put out and the best of men were in darkness wondering if it would ever be light again.

Never did the world seem darker. Economists, who bargained the Master for the price of a slave, ended in the despair of suicide; politicians like Pilate, who washed their hands with water, still found them red with the blood of Deicide; even the Apostles who had heard Him say that He would rise again, doubted that there could ever be a victory after such a defeat.

Just as the despairing of our day look back to what they wrongly think was a golden age, so the Apostles, after the silhouettes of three crosses, were swallowed up in the darkness of Good Friday night, must have looked back to what they thought was their golden age: The Mount of Transfiguration.

How they must have set in contrast those two mountains, the one where His Face did shine as the sun and His garments became white as snow, and the other where His Face was as one struck with leprosy and his only garment the purple patches of His own blood.

How different it all would have been, they must have thought, if the Master had only followed Peter's advice and stayed there in His glory instead of coming down from that hill to set His Face toward Jerusalem and the Cross!

But now it was too late. They had only the memory of a lost kingdom which, like Moses, they had seen with the mind's eye but were never destined to enter.

The glory of the Transfiguration was lost; they had now only the defeat of the crucifix.

Then came Sunday morning at an hour when it yet was dark. A woman steals into the garden, a woman who herself had risen from the dead, for the Master had driven out of her seven devils. If there was anyone who might have been expected to have believed in the Resurrection, it was she.

And yet, on Easter Sunday morning she went to the tomb not to await a Resurrection, but to anoint a dead body, uttering all the while the bitter plaint: "They have taken away my Lord, and I know not where they have laid Him" (John 20:13).

With her whole heart absorbed in this thought, she turned away and lo! Jesus was standing beside her. But it was not Jesus as she had known Him. There was something spiritual, something not of earth in the risen and glorified body.

Some accident of dress or appearance through tear-clouded eyes made her fancy that it was the gardener. In the eager hope that he could explain to her the secret of that empty and angel-haunted grave, she exclaims in an agony of appeal, "Sir, if thou hast taken him hence, tell me where thou hast laid him, and I will take him away" (John 20:15).

Jesus spoke to her one word: "Mary!" He was calling His sheep by name, and there was all heaven in that word.

She looked first to His feet and saw the red scars of the Conqueror of death, and then she uttered but one word, and all earth was in it "Rabboni!"

The birth of the Savior had been announced to a Virgin, the Resurrection from the dead to a convert prostitute — that all the hopeless world might know that they who slew the foe had lost the day. Before the sun had set on that brilliant Easter day, there burned into the hearts of the Apostles and all the world the great lesson: Easter was not within three days of the Transfiguration, it was within three days of Good Friday.

We who believe in the risen Christ cannot share the pessimism and despair of the modern world which feels that this war is the "end of civilization," "the beginning of chaos," "the return to barbarism," and the "decline of the west."

Why do the very ones who once clapped their hands at seeing the Tower of Babel rise, now wring them in dripping despair as it tumbles on their heads?

Why do they, who once danced to the tune of evolution and progress, now sing the lamentations of disillusion?

It is because they started with a very false premise; namely, there is only matter in the universe but no soul, no Divine Purpose, no God.

Now if there is nothing in the universe but matter with its various shapes and forms, then once it begins to disintegrate nothing can stop it.

When an apple begins to rot, it rots through and through; when dynamite explodes, it exhausts itself; when a tree begins to decay, the ravage continues until it falls.

Applying that to our civilization, because the materialists have seen cracks in its walls, they say it now must crumble. Prisoners of the material, they are made captive to hopelessness and despair.

This pessimism we cannot share, because we believe there is something else in the universe besides matter, namely the spirit; and the spirit is never so near a victory as when the flesh is most defeated.

The Master was never so close to His greatest victory as when men built Him a Cross, for Easter Sunday was not within three days of the glory of the Transfiguration, it was within three days of the Cross.

There are three reasons for hope, and therefore for not sharing the defeatism of those, who because they have forgotten their God, have lost the hope of resurrection.

The first reason is this: Moments of great catastrophe are often the eves of great spiritual renaissance.

It was not when the Apostles saw Christ in the transient glory of Transfiguration, but in the ignominy of a tortured man on the Cross, that they were closest to their victory.

Our Divine Lord Himself, speaking of wars, rumors of war, earthquakes, and distress of nations, made the forecast of these calamities the very motive of hope. "But when these things begin to come to pass, look up and lift up your heads because your redemption is at hand" (Luke 21:28).

The reason moments of catastrophe may be the eves of spiritual victory is because it is in those moments of defeat that man's pride is most humbled and his soul thus prepared for the help of God. Israel received her greatest prophets in the hour when all hope seemed gone. The Prodigal was closest to his greatest joy when his substance had been wasted.

It was only when Peter had labored all the night and taken nothing that he was given the miraculous draught of fishes. And in the spiritual life, "the dark night of the soul," the purification of the senses by mortification, is the prelude to the rapturous joys of the spirit.

I believe we are now in such an age, of which Isaias spoke: "I will give thee the treasure of darkness" (Isaiah 45:3).

Darkness may be creative, for it is there that God plants his seeds to grow and his bulbs to flower. It is at night that the sheep which are scattered are gathered into the unity of the sheepfold, when the children come home to their mother, and, the soul back again to God.

Daylight deceives us, but as we awake at night, we get a new sense of values: Darkness seems to tell the awful truth. As the psalmist put it: "Day to day uttereth speech, and night to night sheweth knowledge" (Ps. 18:3).

Night has its wonders as well as day; darkness is not final except to those who are without God.

Applying this to our own time, the beginnings of a new era are often marked by a general barbarization, when the whole historical order is dissolved in a torrent of violence, when Truth in some nations is nailed to a Cross, and in others rejected in a stroke of false broadmindedness.

But since we believe in day as well as in night, and in spirit as well as in matter, we are not without hope in this hour of calamity — for only those who walk in darkness ever see the stars.

We are hopeful not because this is a good world, for presently it is not. Our trust is not in the inherent natural goodness of man, but in the powers of God who can raise him from the dead. Our optimism is based not on "progress," but on its breakdown.

Our modern pagans despair when they become disillusioned about the world. We hope when we begin to be disillusioned about ourselves; and therein is the pathway to repentance and to God, for Easter Sunday was not within three days of the glory of the Transfiguration, it was within three days of the defeat of Good Friday.

The second reason for hope is that in the lifetime of all of us the Church has been more and more emerging into the world from which she was exiled four centuries ago.

Nothing better symbolizes this progressive influence than the manner in which the last three Pontiffs have been crowned as successors of St. Peter.

During the days of the last World War, Benedict XV was crowned in the chapel of the Blessed Mother at the rear of the Basilica of St. Peter's. In the year 1922 his successor, Pius XI moved forward in the Church a few paces and was crowned at the main altar above the very tomb of him who first received the keys of heaven and earth.

But after his coronation Pius XI did something which no Pontiff had done since the year 1870. He walked to the front of St. Peter's, mounted a narrow staircase in the interior of the wall, and then for the first time in half a century, stepped outside of that Church to face the vast throng on the piazza who were awaiting his blessing.

But he did something more than merely step out into that portico; he literally stepped out into the world. The days of defensive warfare were over; from now on there would be a warfare with the breastplate of justice, the shield of faith, the sword of the spirit, and the blessing of Christ.

And just two years ago, when the 261st successor of St. Peter was crowned, he moved even still farther. It was not in the rear of the Basilica, at the altar of the Blessed Mother, that he was crowned; it was not under the dome of the Cathedral and the tomb of St. Peter; it was out on the very portico of the Church itself — more literally still, he was proclaimed a shepherd in the world.

And now as Russia becomes the last hope of nations without faith and is prepared to betray those nations who trusted in her, there will be only one spiritual moral authority left in the world; the only authority which has survived all wars and catastrophes up to this hour and will survive them unto the end.

And as those round about us, who live only on the husks of materialism and mumble their despair, thanks to Christ in His Vicar we live in the hope of a better day, even in an hour that is dark and black, for Easter Sunday was not within three days of the glory of the Transfiguration, it was within three days of the ignominy of Good Friday.

The third and final reason for hope is that the strength of material opposition has no relation to the possibilities of spiritual victory.

When there are only material forces in conflict, the stronger force will invariably win. If on one hand I have a force of fifty pounds, and on the other a force of a thousand pounds, I can be absolutely certain that the force of a thousand pounds will prevail.

But when the contending forces are not both material, but one material and the other spiritual, then the strength of the material opposition, however great it be, is no guarantee of its victory.

A man stands beside Niagara Falls; these mighty waters in an instant could sweep him to death and destruction. But there is within that man an immortal soul made to the image and likeness of God, and being spiritual he can conceive and beget an idea of how to harness those waters and make them minister to the service of man. Materially Niagara should win, actually it loses.

Apply this now to our own times. Let there arise one of the greatest military forces the world has ever seen, let it meet any other material force that is slightly weaker — and barbarism will win; but suppose that that great material force of barbarism is met, not by a foe which attempts to match it in material strength, but by a force that is spiritual, however weak and mean it may seem in the eyes of the world.

The spiritual force will win as the mind of the engineer wins over Niagara. That is why we who believe in Easter and the victory of spirit over matter will not be without hope for America, so long as it trusts in God.

Our hope is grounded not in the magnificent plans for defense, not in increased productiveness of engines of war.

Our hope is grounded in a risen Christ and a revitalized spirituality, for that lesson of the first Easter must be the lesson of our day: Easter was not within three days of the Transfiguration, it was within three days of Good Friday.

The Church in her liturgy this day begs us to seek the things that are above, to rise in our minds with Christ in His Glory as we await the final resurrection of our bodies.

Taking this truly spiritual outlook of the world, and it is the only one that matters, be not disheartened if the externals and accidentals, the trappings and barnacles of the civilization through which we have lived, go down to defeat.

We should face the hard fact that all civilizations, after a certain length of time, become encrusted with a bad philosophy and a worse morals, such as, in our own nation, the primacy of the profit motive over the human, the triumph of divorce over family life, the abandonment of morality and religion in education, the prostitution of the defense of labor by subversive activities.

The effect of this encrustation is to smother the more vital forces within a nation such as religion, morality, sacrifice, the practice of virtue, and the influence of the Church of Christ.

Inside of every egg is potency for new life; but that inner life cannot be free and independent so long as it is enclosed in a shell. In like manner, the vital Christian forces of this nation and of the world cannot assert themselves so long as they are kept imprisoned by the hard shell of materialism and Apostasy from God.

And this war, with all of the horrors, may, under the Providence of God, be the breaking of the shell of modern civilization and the releasing of those spiritual forces which up to this time have been imprisoned by the forces of irreligion.

War is not necessarily the end of a civilization. It may be the beginning of a new and a better world. It can be averted if we discipline ourselves from within and do penance. If we refuse to do that, it may be imposed upon us from without as a chastisement.

But in any case, the shell will be broken and if need be, a war of attrition will be the beginning of our contrition; for Easter Sunday was not within three days of the

Transfiguration, it was within three days of Good Friday.

The world does not yet know it, for the spirit of the world fights only for superficial values. But the conflict of our day is not merely between the barbarism of Germany and the rest of the world, but is part of a larger pattern.

This war will eventually emerge into a struggle of two distinct philosophies of life which may cut across national boundaries with the sharpness of a sword. Each of these philosophies of life will have its own tomb: One tomb will be in Moscow, and the other tomb will be in Jerusalem.

One group of minds in the world will rally about a cadaver, the body of Lenin; the other will rally about the empty tomb of One who was sentenced to death, but fated not to die.

Millions of souls in the world who now hate religion because they hate themselves, will prostrate themselves before an immortality long mortalized and rotted.

Millions of others will lift their eyes to the risen Christ, living in a Church which has survived a hundred crucifixions and a hundred deaths.

And in that conflict between these two forces of evil and good we know not how many swords will be unsheathed or whether they will have to be unsheathed.

We know not whether the conflict will be bloody or unbloody; we know not how far distant in the future lies that battlefield; there is only one thing we do know, and that is, the one thing which will right the world is the one thing which the world today believes to be wrong — the risen Christ and His Church!

ACKNOWLEDGMENTS

I want to thank Almighty God for the health of mind, body, and spirit to put together these reflections.

To my good wife, Isabel, my children, and my grandchildren, who keep me young at heart and are truly a blessing from God. Thank you for sharing in my joy.

I wish to express my gratitude to members of the Archbishop Fulton John Sheen Foundation in Peoria, Illinois — in particular, to the Most Rev. Daniel R. Jenky, C.S.C., Bishop of Peoria, for your leadership and fidelity to the cause of Sheen's canonization and the creation of this book.

To Julie Enzenberger, O.C.V., who repeated to me time and time again Sheen's words: "Believe the incredible, and you can do the impossible."

To the staff and volunteers at Sophia Institute Press for their invaluable assistance in helping to publish the writings of Archbishop Fulton J. Sheen.   I am indebted to them for this great work.

To the many seminarians, priests, religious, bishops, and cardinals I have met during this journey. Always remember the words of Archbishop Sheen that "The priest is not his own."

To the tens of thousands of people I have met in my travels, giving presentations about Archbishop Fulton J. Sheen at parishes, conferences, universities, high schools, church groups, and even pubs: thank you for sharing with me your many "Sheen Stories." I truly cherish each one of them.

And lastly, to Archbishop Fulton J. Sheen, whose teachings on prayer, the sacraments, our Lord's Passion, and His Seven Last Words continue to inspire me to love God more and to appreciate the gift of the Church. His teachings and his encouragement to make a Holy Hour each day has been a true gift in my life. May I be so blessed as to imitate Archbishop Sheen's love for the saints, the sacraments, the Eucharist, and for the Mother of God. May the Good Lord grant him a very high place in Heaven!

— Al Smith

ABOUT THE AUTHOR

Fulton J. Sheen

(1895–1979)

Fulton John Sheen was born in El Paso, Illinois, in 1895. In high school, he won a three-year university scholarship, but he turned it down to pursue a vocation to the priesthood. He attended St. Viator College Seminary in Illinois and St. Paul Seminary in Minnesota. In 1919, he was ordained a priest for the Diocese of Peoria, Illinois. He earned a licentiate in sacred theology and a bachelor of canon law at the Catholic University of America and a doctorate at the Catholic University of Louvain, Belgium.

Sheen received numerous teaching offers but declined them in obedience to his bishop and became an assistant pastor in a rural parish. Having thus tested his obedience, the bishop later permitted him to teach at the Catholic University of America and at St. Edmund's College in Ware, England, where he met G. K. Chesterton, whose weekly BBC radio broadcast inspired Sheen's later NBC broadcast, The Catholic Hour (1930–1952).

In 1952, Sheen began appearing on ABC in his own series; Life Is Worth Living. Despite being given a time slot that forced him to compete with Milton Berle and Frank Sinatra, the dynamic Sheen enjoyed enormous success and in 1954 reach tens of millions of viewers, non-Catholics as well as Catholics.

When asked by Pope Pius XII how many converts he had made, Sheen responded, "Your Holiness, I have never counted them. I am always afraid if I did count them, I might think I made them, instead of the Lord."

Sheen gave annual Good Friday homilies at New York's St. Patrick's Cathedral, led numerous retreats for priests and religious, and preached at summer conferences in England.

"If you want people to stay as they are," he said, "tell them what they want to hear. If you want to improve them, tell them what they should know." This he did, not only in his preaching but also in the more than ninety books he wrote. His Peace of Soul was sixth on the New York Times best-seller list.

Sheen served as auxiliary bishop of New York (1951–1966) and as bishop of Rochester (1966–1969).

Two of his great loves were for the Blessed Mother and the Eucharist. He made a daily holy hour before the Blessed Sacrament, from which he drew strength and inspiration to preach the gospel and in the presence of which he prepared his homilies. "I beg [Christ] every day to keep me strong physically and alert mentally in order to preach His gospel and proclaim His Cross and Resurrection," he said. "I am so happy doing this that I sometimes feel that when I come to the good Lord in Heaven, I will take a few days' rest and then ask Him to allow me to come back again to this earth to do some more work."

Sheen also said that "the greatest love story of all time is contained in a tiny white host." This was the love that transformed him. His daily Eucharistic Holy Hour was legendary. From the day of his ordination to the day of his death, Sheen spent an hour a day praying in the presence of the Blessed Sacrament. From his office desk, through an open door, he could gaze upon the tabernacle at all times. His union with Christ enabled him to more fully, more accurately and more convincingly lead others to Christ in all he said and did. Sheen was a man of many talents and accomplishments, but it was Christ who enabled him to use them in the best ways.

The good Lord called Fulton Sheen home in 1979. His television broadcasts, now on tape, and his books continue his earthly work of winning souls for Christ. Sheen's cause for canonization was opened in 2002. In 2012, Pope Benedict XVI declared him "Venerable." In 2019, Pope Francis approved a miracle attributed to the intercession of the Venerable Fulton Sheen, clearing the way for his beatification.

Books Available Through Bishop Sheen Today Publishing

The Rainbow of Sorrow

The Seven Last Words

Calvary and the Mass

Love One Another

The Cross and the Beatitudes

The Cross and the Crisis

Love One Another

Victory Over Vice

The Seven Virtues

For God and Country

God and War

The Divine Verdict

God Love You

The Seven Last Words Explained

The Priest Is Not His Own

The Cross and the Crib

Philosophies at War

The Seven Last Words of Christ Explained

Father, Forgive Them for They Know Not What They Do.

This Day Thou Shall Be with Me in Paradise

Woman Behold Your Son; Behold Your Mother

My God! My God! Why Hast Thou Forsaken Me?

I Thirst

It is Finished

Father Into Your Hands I Commend My Spirit

Liberty, Equality and Fraternity

Missions and the World Crisis

Seven Words to the Cross

Seven Pillars of Peace

The Holy Hour Prayer Book

Seven Words of Jesus & Mary

www.bishopsheentoday.com